About Mammals

About Mammals

A Guide for Children

Cathryn Sill

Illustrated by John Sill

McGraw Hill SRA

Columbus, OH

For the One who created mammals.

—*Genesis* 1:24

First published in the United States under the title ABOUT MAMMALS: A GUIDE FOR CHILDREN by Cathryn Sill, illustrated By John C. Sill. Text Copyright © 1997, 1999 by Cathryn P. Sill. Illustrations Copyright (c) 1991, 1997, 2013 by John C. Sill. Published by arrangement with Peachtree Publishers.

SRAonline.com

Mc Graw Hill **SRA**

Copyright © 2008 by SRA/McGraw-Hill.

All rights reserved. Except as permitted under the United States Copyright Act, no part of this publication may be reproduced or distributed in any form or by any means, or stored in a database or retrieval system, without the prior written permission of the publisher, unless otherwise indicated.

Printed in the United States of America.

Send all inquiries to:
SRA/McGraw-Hill
4400 Easton Commons
Columbus, OH 43219-6188

ISBN 978-0-07-612515-9
MHID 0-07-612515-7

11 12 13 MER 25 24 23

The McGraw-Hill Companies

About Mammals

Mammals have hair.

PLATE 1
Raccoon

John Sill

They may have thick fur,

PLATE 2
Musk Oxen

sharp quills,

PLATE 3
Porcupine

John Sill

or only a few stiff whiskers.

PLATE 4
Walrus

Baby mammals drink milk from their mothers.

PLATE 5
Bison

John Gill

Some mammals are born helpless.

PLATE 6
White-footed Mice

Others can move about on their own
soon after they are born.

PLATE 7
E*lk*

John Sill

Mammals may run,

PLATE 8
Pronghorns

John Sill

climb,

PLATE 9
Red Squirrel

John Zill

swim,

PLATE 10
Blue Whale

John Zill

or fly.

PLATE 11
Big Brown Bat

John Sill

Mammals eat meat,

PLATE 12
Bobcat

John Sill

plants,

PLATE 13
Pika

or both.

PLATE 14
Black Bear

They may live in cold, icy places…

PLATE 15
Arctic Fox

John Gill

hot, dry deserts…

PLATE 16
Blacktail Jackrabbit

John Sill

or wet marshes.

PLATE 17
Muskrat

John Sill

It is important to protect mammals where they live.

PLATE 18
Humans, Raccoon, Gray Squirrel, White-tailed Deer

Afterword

PLATE 1
Hair in its different forms protects mammals in ways uniquely adapted for each species. Raccoons are found in each of the lower forty-eight states.

PLATE 2
Musk Oxen live in the cold Arctic region. They have a thick outer coat of long guard hairs covering a dense undercoat that keeps them warm in frigid temperatures.

PLATE 3
Porcupines have sharp stiff quills on their backs and tails. The quills are loosely attached and will come off and stick into an enemy's body.

PLATE 4
Some marine mammals have only a few coarse whiskers. Walruses use their sensitive, bristly whiskers to forage for food on the ocean floor. They eat snails, clams, crabs, and shrimp.

PLATE 5
Bison, also called American Buffalo, were nearly hunted to extinction in the late 1800s. They are now protected and their numbers have slowly increased. Bison are the largest land animals in North America.

PLATE 6
White-footed Mice babies are weaned when they are about three weeks old.

PLATE 7
Baby Elk must be able to run very fast soon after birth to avoid danger from predators (animals that eat other animals). Newborn Elk can stand up about twenty minutes after birth.

PLATE 8
Pronghorns can run over fifty miles per hour for several miles. They are the fastest mammals in North America.

PLATE 9
Red Squirrels are small, noisy tree squirrels. Squirrels are rodents. Rodents' teeth continue to grow all their lives. These animals must gnaw a great deal of the time to keep their teeth worn down.

PLATE 10
Blue Whales are the largest animals in the world. They grow up to 100 feet and may weigh 200 tons.

PLATE 11
Bats are the only mammals that truly fly. Big Brown Bats have a body length of $4\frac{1}{8}$ to 5 inches. They can fly at speeds up to forty miles per hour. Bats are very beneficial because many of them feed on insects.

PLATE 12
Though Bobcats can kill animals larger than themselves, they hunt mainly rabbits, squirrels, and mice.

PLATE 13
In midsummer, Pikas begin to gather plants which they pile into stacks to dry in the sun. They store these haystacks for winter food. Pikas do not hibernate in winter, but move about in tunnels they dig.

PLATE 14
Black Bears are the most common bear in North America. They will eat many different things including roots, berries, insects, and small mammals.

PLATE 15
The white winter coats of Arctic Foxes change to brown in summer. This camouflage or protective coloration allows them to hide from both predators and prey.

PLATE 16
Blacktail Jackrabbits are not really rabbits, but hares. Hares do not dig burrows and their young are born fully furred with their eyes open. Jackrabbits have very keen hearing which helps them to avoid predators.

PLATE 17
Muskrats have a tail that is flattened from side to side. They use this flattened tail to guide them as they swim. Muskrats build their domed houses in water using marsh vegetation.

PLATE 18
One of the primary dangers to mammals is habitat destruction. We must be responsible to maintain an environment where mammals are provided space, shelter, food, and water.
Can you find the animal in this picture that is not a mammal?

Also in the About... series

About Birds
About Reptiles
About Amphibians
About Insects
About Fish
About Arachnids
About Crustaceans
About Mollusks

Fred Eldredge, Creative Image Photography

Cathryn Sill, a former elementary school teacher, is the author of the acclaimed ABOUT... series. With her husband John and her brother-in-law Ben Sill, she coauthored the popular bird-guide parodies, A FIELD GUIDE TO LITTLE-KNOWN AND SELDOM-SEEN BIRDS OF NORTH AMERICA, ANOTHER FIELD GUIDE TO LITTLE-KNOWN AND SELDOM-SEEN BIRDS OF NORTH AMERICA, and BEYOND BIRDWATCHING, all from Peachtree Publishers.

John Sill is a prize-winning and widely published wildlife artist who illustrated the ABOUT... series and coauthored the FIELD GUIDES and BEYOND BIRDWATCHING. A native of North Carolina, he holds a B.S. in Wildlife Biology from North Carolina State University.

The Sills live and work in Franklin, North Carolina.